AF377996

JOSIANE FORTIN

Mine Your Brain

288 Insightful Questions to Live Your Best Life

This book was professionally typeset on Reedsy.
Find out more at reedsy.com

Contents

Mine Your Gray Cells

"Super thinking is really asking yourself to look beyond the surface answers and to ask deeper questions."
- *Brooke Castillo*

Your mind contains gold & diamond. It's available 24/7, and you can dig in to find all your answers. You can transform your life and generate revolutionary ideas and solutions if you build your thinking skills, and it starts with asking more powerful questions.

Imagine a miner sifting the bottom of the river hoping to find gold. He knows the difference between this precious metal and the shiny iron pirate. In your brain, there are thoughts that shine, that seem true. However, these thoughts are often simply opinions, not facts. Once you identify them, you can decide to replace them with new ones that are worth gold instead. Thoughts that brighten your day, that motivate you, that soothe you.

This book will help you mine your own wealthy property, your brain, which is the most powerful tool on Earth. Learn how to take full advantage of this priceless resource you were born with.

While we often turn to others to figure out our lives, we should rely more on what we can find inside ourselves. You instinctively know what is best for you. By turning inward to find our own answers, you use a power few will dare to master. Find out how to answer your questions and stop depending on others to tell you your truth.

If you are reading this book, it is probably because you want an extraordinary life. Achieving this requires informed and purposeful thinking. Selecting the right questions will help you think at a higher level. For example, a fruitful question opens up possibilities, such as, *"How can I do this?"* Whereas an unfruitful question does not lead to progress, but a feeling of helplessness, such as, *"Why is this happening to me?"* Can you see the difference it makes?

A fruitful question will help you get creative in finding solutions, while an unfruitful question lets you spin in circles. This is the reason the quality of your questions influences the quality of your reasoning, and therefore, your results. Focus on solutions rather than digging into the problem, meaning don't look for what is wrong with you (hint: nothing), or why this situation is happening. Instead, find questions that will help you figure out what to do from where you are right at this moment, no matter how difficult. Then, act on the best ideas, see the results you get, and fine-tune if necessary.

Years ago, I started a file to accumulate all the brilliant questions that I wanted to ask myself. As I compiled an inventory for my personal use, I realized how powerful they would be for others, too. I am sharing this work with you today.

Outstanding Thinking

"The quality of your life is a direct reflection of the quality of the questions you are asking yourself."

- Tony Robbins

Outstanding thinking is what will make you stand out from the crowd. This skill will help you innovate and build the life you want by pushing the limits on what has been done. You will manage your brain to direct your thoughts in the most productive way.

When you up-level your thinking, you realize value is not created by regurgitating information you had to memorize in school to do well on the test. It's about finding your own truth and creating intellectual property that can serve the world.

There is no right or wrong answer when you are creating. You won't get an A or a B-. There is no grading. There is just you and your life, what you want to do with it and what you want to leave behind. The legacy you are creating with your brain.

Of course, to help this process, adding input to your brain is essential. This information is the foundation on which you can build your new ideas. You can mix and match your knowledge from different fields to create an amazing new product or service. You can decide to go against commonly accepted principles to explore how the world could differ from what you've been told it is.

You have accumulated so much information in your lifetime, either through experiences or formal learning activities, that it is time to trust that the answers are inside of you. Although external information is essential, it is not the aim of the outstanding thinking process and if you are looking for specific facts, Google it. But you alone can decide what meaning you want to give to your life, and what is best for your situation and your ambitions.

It's possible that what you're trying to accomplish was never done, or not quite the unique way that can work for you. If you are the first, you can't follow others there. Recycling is effective for plastic packaging, not so much for thoughts. If you merely rely on concepts currently available, you might end up recycling obsolete materials, perpetuating the misjudgments of the past. Why would you choose to do that? Rather, decide to build a legacy with fresh intellectual property.

If you keep relying on others to bring you answers and decisions, you are not being intentional about your life. You are just following the opinions of others, shifting direction each time you hear a fresh piece of advice. There are many ways to get to your end goal and your brain has all the answers you need.

Then, during your outstanding thinking sessions, mix your current knowledge with your experiences and your dreams. This blend will give birth to new opinions and ideas. The more you practice pulling answers from your brain, the better you'll become at it. It's a skill you build for life. Sit down and force your brain to come up with 10 ideas on any topic and let your inner wisdom come through. The information you get may not come to you shaped as a specific answer, but it might inspire you to take the next step.

Developing your ability to think at a higher-level is to become a notable resource for your colleagues, your family, and your friends. If you train week after week to come up with ideas that are innovative and actionable within the framework of a specific project or problem, your contribution will provide an incredible value for everyone, yourself included.

How to use these prompts

"If you change the quality of your thinking, you change the quality of your life."

- Brian Tracy

To access your inner wisdom, develop your thinking skills by working on it every week. Only with practice and time will you increase your ability. Set some time to think in your schedule to mine your brain. Start with just a few minutes if you have to. Keep at it.

If you already journal frequently, you can supercharge this habit by using one prompt every day. You could decide to work on the same question for some time in order to dig deep into the issue you are most concerned with at the moment. This process will allow your brain to come up with so many ideas about this specific area of interest that it will propel you where you want to be.

Another way is to pick a question at random, and get all your thoughts down on a piece of paper. This method will open your mind to areas where you did not think you could or wanted to improve. You could uncover unexpected treasures.

If you do not wish to journal, pick any notebook to record

your ideas. Write the question of your choosing on top of the page and add the date. You will see how far you have come by seeing how many actions you have taken after your outstanding thinking sessions.

Writing your answers down is essential to dig deep into your mind. There is some magic about writing your thoughts on a piece of paper rather than on a computer screen. Researchers have found that there are many benefits to handwriting. Putting pen to paper activates a distinct part of your brain. No matter the scientific explanation behind this, what is important to remember is that it is effective. Try it for yourself.

If you get stuck during your session, there are some strategies you can use. First, pretend that you live in a perfect world. In that imagined situation, what would the answer be? Sometimes, we get confused because the options society offers us, available and reasonable, are not appealing to us. No wonder we then pretend we don't know what to do. If you get to pick between three horrible options, of course you would get puzzled. Get out of the commonly accepted rules for now and see what new ideas come up for you.

Second, you could pretend that you are talking with a best friend, a coach, a therapist, or any person who you respect and admire. Do both sides of the conversation. Start by explaining the problem as you see it. Then, change characters and make up that counselor's answer. This role-play helps you access your own knowledge.

Third, you can do the opposite and pretend that it is a friend asking for your help. What would you tell them in that exact situation? Often, the answer is easier said than done, so by removing yourself from the issue, you will more freely access your truth. By pretending that you won't be the one implementing the suggestions, you remove the fear that could stop you from thinking freely.

I have used these three techniques to help me when I got stuck. In fact, I have often imagined talking to a life coach I admire, Brooke Castillo. I pretended she was there to answer my questions and, to my surprise, I was coming up with fabulous answers when I did not know what to do a few minutes earlier.

As you read over the questions to select the one you wish to work on, never forget that you can tweak them to better represent your own situation. Come up with really high-quality questions for problems that you're having, for ideas that you want to create, and then listen to yourself for the answer. I only share in this booklet some questions to get you started and inspired. Don't stop there.

I did not get through all these questions myself and I don't recommend that you do that. The point is to ask the right question at the right time, and then act on what you decide. What do you want to discover?

Are you living a deliberate life, or are you living on default?

Thinking Prompts

"A genius is simply one who has taken full possession of his own mind and directed it toward objectives of his own choosing, without permitting outside influences to discourage or mislead him."

- Napoleon Hill

This is it! Here are all the high-level questions I have compiled, ready for you to use. Dig answers in your brain, take charge of your life and live your best life.

Upgrading Your Life

If you are looking to get more out of life, this section is for you.

1. How can I get more happiness into my life? More joy? More laughter?
2. How do I make my life more fun?
3. How can I travel more?
4. What are 25 things I want to do or experience before I die?
5. Where do I want to be in 5, 10 or 20 years and what can I do today to get there?
6. What is my biggest dream for the future, and what can I do today to get closer to it?
7. How can I enjoy my life more?
8. Who do I need to become to have what I want?
9. Who do I want to be in one year and how can I get there?
10. Who could help me have bigger dreams?
11. If I pretend my life right now is just a 3 out of 10, what would an 8 look like?
12. What would my life be like if it were 10 times better than it is now?
13. What can I do to create more fun experiences in my day-to-day life?
14. What minor changes can I implement today to get closer

to my ideal lifestyle? What is that ideal lifestyle?
15. What can I do to feel satisfied and balanced?
16. What do I really want to do with my life?
17. What do I spend the most time thinking about?
18. What are the problems I need to solve right now?
19. What is helping me achieve the success that I want?
20. What are 10 ideas for vacations I want to take?
21. What would a day in my dream life look like?
22. What is possible for my life?
23. How would I act if I wasn't "middle class" in my head?
24. What do I need to do differently to see the results I want?
25. What do I need to be focusing on in order to create the exact life I want?
26. Why do I want to stay in this comfort zone?
27. If anything was possible, what kind of life would I create for myself?
28. How can I create a circle of friends who inspire, lift, and help me get to the next version of me?
29. If I were to achieve an amazing goal this year, how would I succeed?
30. What would be a life that I would love in all its aspects: relationships, work, money, spiritual life, possessions, home, family, achievements, health, education, book time, hobbies, travel?
31. If I were to succeed beyond my wildest dreams, what would my life look like?
32. How can I improve the world?
33. What do I need to know to have the success I dream of?
34. What value can I create that nobody else can?
35. What would I believe and do if I already achieved my goal?
36. What does living well mean to me?

37. What is my idea of fun? Not what I think society's idea of fun is.
38. Who do I want to be in 5 years and what can I do today to get closer to that vision?
39. How do I want people to remember me when I'm dead?
40. What would a perfect week look like?
41. What is missing in my life to make it even better?
42. What would bring more joy to my life right now?
43. How can I inspire others?
44. How can I become the role model I want to be for my kids? Or for my community?
45. What do I believe is stopping me from achieving my dream life?
46. Who do I want to be?
47. What do I most want to accomplish in my life and why?
48. What do I want to create in this lifetime?

Discovering Your Aspiration

Self-awareness is the foundation for making decisions that are aligned with who you are and where you want to go.

1. What do I aspire to?
2. What do I do when time seems to fly by?
3. What would my dream job be?
4. Does my dream job exist, or can I create it in my company?
5. What do I look forward to doing when I am off work or on vacation?
6. If money were no object, what kind of work would I like to do?
7. If my boss gave me a year off to work in the community, what field would I choose?
8. Are there any courses I would like to take at a college or continuing education center?
9. What images come to mind when I imagine myself in an ideal job?
10. What is my intuition telling me right now about an ideal job?
11. Is there an action that my thinking is driving me to?
12. Is there an exciting, fascinating or interesting idea that I want to pursue?

13. What would my life be if money was not a consideration?
14. What kind of lifestyle would have if money was plentiful?
15. If anything was allowed and possible, what would be my dream job?
16. Why do I believe this unwanted thought to be true?
17. What results from this unwanted thought?
18. What if the opposite of this unwanted thought is true?
19. Why do I choose to believe this unwanted thought?
20. What would I do if it wasn't currently impossible?
21. How can I use my strengths to achieve my dream?

Growing Personally

Personal development is key to being a master of your mind and your emotions.

1. How can I show more of my light?
2. How do I balance the rational and the spiritual sides of me?
3. What thoughts make me feel unstoppable?
4. Why am I choosing to believe I can't identify my blind spots?
5. Why does this situation make me sad?
6. How can I be a better ally (to women, to LGBTQIA+, to people of color, to first nations, to anyone different and less privileged)
7. What makes me angry and is it a reflection of myself?
8. What positive thoughts would I like to believe?
9. What thoughts are not serving me and how can I let them go?
10. What actions must I take in the next month?
11. What actions must I stop taking for the next month?
12. What can I do to follow my intuition better?
13. What are 10 awesome ideas for me?

Reaching Your Goals

Once you have a goal in mind, make it bigger and rise to the challenge.

1. How do I make my goal happen?
2. Did someone reach a similar goal and would her strategy work for me?
3. Do I hold high expectations for myself? How has that helped me and blocked me?
4. What would be the solution in an ideal world?
5. How can I structure my environment so that I am more likely to take action on my priorities?
6. If anything were possible, what would my goal be?
7. What can I do when I feel tempted to procrastinate on my goal?
8. What kind of person achieves this goal? How can I become more like that?
9. How will I feel when I reach this goal? How can I feel this way right now?
10. What tools and strengths can I apply to reach this goal?
11. What steps can I take today to get closer to my goal?
12. How can I develop the skills I want?
13. Who do I know that could help me with this goal?

14. What positive consequences will I get when I reach this goal?
15. What do I fear losing while working on this goal?
16. Is this goal aligned with my life's plan and my values?
17. What actions do I need to take to ensure the result I want will happen?
18. How can I become better known, attract media attention, stand out?
19. What do I need to learn to make my goal happen?
20. What can I do to write my book faster?
21. What would make this project go smoother?
22. How to think bigger in this project?
23. How can we get to the finish line sooner?
24. What is preventing me from taking this decision? What are my excuses?
25. How do I stay connected to my goal and fuel my motivation?
26. What actions do I need to take to get working towards my goal?
27. Why am I procrastinating on this task?
28. Who do I need to become in order to make my goal possible?
29. What do I need to stop being or doing in order to make my goal possible?
30. How to make bigger progress?
31. Why do I think I won't achieve this goal this month?
32. Who do I need to be to accomplish my goals this year?
33. What goals am I ready to commit to in the next year?
34. How do I create more of the feeling that I want?
35. What excuses do I have not to work on my goal? And what can I do about them?

36. What actions should I take in the next 12 months?

18

Forging Habits

Routines can be helpful to keep your energy high and results higher.

1. How can I make myself enjoy journaling and do it every day?
2. How can I exercise more?
3. What could help me eat healthier?
4. What habit would I like to develop? How could I take action today to make this a reality?
5. How can I increase my energy?
6. How do I stay in the present moment?
7. What is preventing me from taking action right now?
8. How can I better organize my life?
9. How can I make it easier to follow up on this habit?
10. How can I make mediation part of my routine?
11. What would be the best time of day to read a book chapter?

Building Your Wealth

Money is good in the hands of people of integrity and generosity. You deserve prosperity.

1. How can I earn more money?
2. How can I create passive income?
3. How can I save 20% of my gross salary?
4. How can I bring my credit cards to 0?
5. What do I need to learn to be debt-free?
6. How can I get rid of my debts?
7. What actions do I need to take to get out of debt?
8. What are the most valuable decisions to get to where I want to be?
9. How do I find my wealth within me?
10. What actions would allow me to buy my dream home?
11. What do I believe to be true about money? Do I want to keep this belief?
12. What is preventing me from giving more money to causes I believe in?
13. How can I make 1M$ a year?
14. How can I make as much money as I want?
15. How can I believe it is possible for me to make $1M?
16. What thoughts have become my default programming in

my finances?

17. What excuses do I have not to save money? And what can I do about them?
18. What would I do if I believed that money was easy?
19. What is my plan to earn more money?

Improving Your Career

Here are questions to propel your career or business.

1. How do I show my boss I am ready for a promotion?
2. How can I create my dream business?
3. What can I do to grow more and faster?
4. What are the top 5 areas my boss wants me to focus on or areas that bring the most value to my business?
5. What is the scariest thing I have to do to 10x my business / income / sales?
6. What do I need to learn to get to the next level?
7. What does the next level look like for me? Can I dream even bigger?
8. How can I increase my value in the job market?
9. What are the most valuable tasks to get to where I want to be?
10. How do I stop stressing out or overworking ?
11. What should be my next career move and who do I need to be to get there?
12. What actions do I need to take to get out of a job I dislike?
13. What actions do I need to take to get my dream job?
14. How can I position myself as an expert in my field?
15. What thoughts have become my default programming in

my career?

16. What is the value I will enjoy creating in the world & who would I like to create it for?
17. What does being an entrepreneur mean to me?
18. What excuses do I have not to start a business? And what can I do about them?
19. How do I motivate my team?
20. What can I do to feel more motivated by my career?
21. What are 10 awesome ideas for my company?
22. What is the value that I can create for my customers?

Selling Effectively

Selling your ideas is crucial to lead. Selling products and services creates value for all involved in the transaction.

1. How do I get to being totally in love with my work/creations/novels?
2. How can I get more visibility for my achievements?
3. What am I afraid of when I sell?
4. What does my client need and how can I help them get what they want?
5. How do I get more people to sign up for our webinar next month?
6. How do I build a stronger brand?
7. What do I need to do to have record business revenues this semester?
8. How can I get more people to sign up for my newsletter?
9. What are 10 awesome ideas for my clients?
10. How can I make my products visible in the marketplace?

Strengthening Relationships

With reliable partnerships, you exchange the love, the friendship, and the help needed to thrive.

1. What can I do to become a better friend to people around me?
2. How can I love Person X more? What is preventing me from loving them more? What does it mean and what can I do about it?
3. How do I exude something worth following?
4. How would I like to show up as a partner, a spouse, a parent, an employee, or a boss?
5. What actions do I need to take to deepen my relationship with my partner?
6. What actions do I need to take to heal my heart ache?
7. What is preventing me from achieving my dream relationship?
8. What do I believe to be true about my partner? Do I want to keep this belief?
9. What thoughts have become my default programming in my relationship?
10. How can I enjoy my children more, play more with them, be with them?

11. How do I want to feel in my relationship?
12. What do I want to receive? What do I want to give?
13. How can I better manage my anger?
14. How can you show up as the most amazing parent?
15. How do I motivate my kid to play outside?
16. How do I motivate my partner to contribute more?
17. What do I believe about the people in my life (spouse, kids, coworkers, etc)?

Loving Yourself

When you love yourself, you get rid of many limiting beliefs. You must know you deserve more to get it.

1. How can I love myself more?
2. What have I had enough of?
3. If I believed I was the type of person who always gets what she wants, what would I do?
4. What is one task that I could let go of or do less often?
5. What did I have to do as a kid to please my parents? How has that influenced my behavior today?
6. What actions do I need to take to love myself a bit more today?
7. What actions do I need to take to heal my depression?
8. How can I better manage my anxiety?
9. What actions do I need to take to increase my self-confidence
10. What feeling do I want more of, and how can I create that for myself?
11. What would help me feel more love for myself?
12. What do I love about myself?
13. What activities give me pleasure and joy? How can I do more of that?

14. How can I trust myself more?
15. How do I create more self-love?
16. What am I waiting for to love myself?

Healing Your Past

Strop dragging negative feelings into the present. Free yourself.

1. How can I rewrite my past to focus on the positives?
2. What do I believe to be true about my mother or my father? Do I want to keep these beliefs?
3. What can I do today to fix what I consider a past mistake? Why is it a mistake in the first place?
4. Why am I frustrated?
5. Why do I feel stressed?
6. What is my path to peace?
7. Why don't I want to make mistakes?
8. Why do I want to be perfect?
9. What thoughts have become my default programming in my past?
10. What would it take for me to feel good right now?
11. How can I reconnect with my inner child?

Facing Challenges

Know in your heart that you can overcome any challenge.

1. Who do I want to be in this difficult situation?
2. What should I be learning thanks to this challenge?
3. How can I reduce stress as much as possible?
4. What would someone I admire do in this situation?
5. How do I want to show up in this challenging situation?
6. What actions do I need to take to get out of this challenging situation?
7. What other solutions could help with this problem?
8. Can I look at this problem differently?
9. Is there a way to circumvent this challenge?

Solving Your Problems

Believe in your ability to deal with any issue you might encounter.

1. How will I know if I solved the problem?
2. How will I feel once I solve this problem?
3. How will my life (or my company, my team, etc.) be different when the problem is solved?
4. How do I see myself when the problem is solved?
5. What would (someone I look up to) do?
6. What would I do if I knew what to do?
7. How is this issue that I'm currently dealing with for me instead of against me?

Losing Weight

This section applies only if you decide your current size dissatisfies you.

1. How would having the perfect figure change my life?
2. What foods do I enjoy?
3. How would I feel at my ideal weight?
4. What would I look like at my ideal weight?
5. What kinds of clothes would I wear?
6. What can my body do with ease?
7. What kinds of physical activities do I enjoy?
8. What can I do when I feel tempted to eat food I planned not to eat?
9. What do I need to stop being / doing in order to make my goal possible?
10. What am I trying to forget when I overeat?
11. What emotion am I trying to avoid by eating?
12. What do I need to do differently to see the results I want?
13. How do I change my focus from food? What do I want to refocus on?
14. What excuses do I have to eat too much food? And what can I do about them?
15. How am I going to figure out this overeating problem?

16. Why do I think I need to lose weight?
17. How is my extra weight helping me right now?

Knowing Yourself

Connecting to your identity is crucial to taking the best path. Indeed, self-awareness is essential, because if you want to make the best decisions in your life, the ones that will bring you joy and pride, you must first know who you are. Otherwise, you are leaving it up to luck.

1. Who am I?
2. Who am I living for?
3. How do I want to spend my life?
4. What is the biggest lack in my life?
5. What brings me the most joy in my life right now?
6. What did I want to be when I grew up?
7. What is my largest time commitment?
8. What are my top 3 values?
9. What do I feel guilty about doing? About not doing?
10. What do I worry about often?
11. Why do I sabotage myself?
12. What would I try if it weren't too crazy, scary, selfish?
13. What are 5 hobbies I'd like to try?
14. What skills would I like to have?
15. What countries do I wish to visit?
16. What classes would I pick if I went back to school?

17. What are my top 5 qualities?
18. What are my top 5 negative traits?
19. Who do I admire?
20. What do I believe about God?
21. What do I believe happens after death?
22. Are there things I stop myself from doing because I am afraid?
23. What is my biggest fear and, if I choose to, how can I get over it?
24. What do I believe to be true about me? Do I want to keep this belief?
25. How much control do I believe I have over my life and do I want to keep believing this?
26. How do I see myself and why?
27. What would I choose to believe if I could believe anything?
28. How would I like to see myself?
29. What are the 5 things I could get rid of today?
30. What do I need to do and to be to see myself in the best light?
31. How can I be authentic?

Conclusion

This book was to guide you to find your own answers through the suggested questions, but now it's time to step up your game by coming up with your own high-level, powerful questions.

Don't stop at what you have read in those pages; ask your own brain to come up with the best, most critical questions for your life. Use them in your thinking sessions. Zoom in on your specific goals and seek the questions that will help you rise to the occasion.

Be inspired to create your own questions. You can try to make different versions to solve the same problem. For example, here is a list specific questions for a salesperson:

1. How do I increase customer retention?
2. What would be the best way to get more customers?
3. Why do we lose our best customers?
4. Why do so many customers leave the company?
5. How do we attract loyal customers?

These questions all focus on the same business issue, but with a different angle.

If the questions don't come, trick yourself by wondering what someone else might suggest. What would you come up with if you knew? Finding the most compelling questions is an exceptional skill to develop to get to the success you dream of.

37

About the Author

Josiane Fortin loves to provide value and entertainment to readers. That's why she write in different genres: non-fiction, science fiction, and fantasy.

She is Canadian and has lived in Mexico and the United States.

She thanks you for purchasing this. It is a pleasure for her to tell stories and your purchase encourages me to continue my creative work.

Let's keep in touch!

You can connect with me on:
- http://josianefortin.ca/en/writer
- https://ko-fi.com/jfortin
- On YouTube @Upturn Community

Subscribe to my newsletter:
- https://mailchi.mp/d7d6e72c9f20/habitcreationworksheet

Also by Josiane Fortin

The One-Year Plan: How To Build Your Empire One Brick At a Time By Creating A Personal Plan
A step by step guide to effectively create your personal annual plan!

- Specific categories to guide your thinking

- Examples of goals to inspire you and help you step out of your comfort zone

- A method to select and prioritize your goals

- Help for crafting action-oriented goals that are achievable

- Motivate you to take action

This book is designed for those who have their head full of dreams, but that feel they are not moving fast enough towards reaching them.

A process that can be renewed each year to get the most out of this proven technique.

587 Affirmations for Women: Use the Power of Affirmations to Change Your Life

Do you want to harness the power of affirmations to improve your life?

This booklet is for you. It offers 587 affirmations that cover all the important areas of your life: love, health, family, career, money, self-esteem, goals, and more.

A list of ready-made affirmations, for any occasions and for every situation in your life!

Simply be inspired by the statements and select the ones that suit you.

Adapt your favorite affirmations to your situation to make them even more powerful!